The Marta Poems

"This is what you do.
You start with nothing and make whatever you can.
If you lose it, you start over and try something new."

~ Marta

The Marta Poems

The Marta Poems

Susan J. Atkinson

720 Sixth Street, Unit #5
New Westminster, BC
V3L 3C5
CANADA

The Marta Poems

Title: The Marta Poems
Author: Susan J. Atkinson
Publisher: Silver Bow Publishing
Cover Art: "Dandelion Fluff" by Susan J. Atkinson"
Cover Layout and Design: Candice James
Editing: Candice James

All rights reserved including the right to reproduce or translate this book or any portions thereof, in any form without the permission of the publisher. Except for the use of short passages for review purposes, no part of this book may be reproduced, in part or in whole, or transmitted in any form or by any means, either by means electronically or mechanically, including photocopying, recording, or any information or storage retrieval system without prior permission in writing from the publisher or a licence from the Canadian Copyright Collective Agency (Access Copyright).

www.silverbowpublishing.com
info@silverbowpublishing.com
ISBN: 978-1-77403-098-1 paperback
ISBN: 978-1-77403-099-8 electronic book
© Silver Bow Publishing

Library and Archives Canada Cataloguing in Publication

Title: The Marta poems / by Susan J. Atkinson.
Names: Atkinson, Susan J., 1964- author.
Identifiers: Canadiana (print) 20200254197 | Canadiana (ebook) 20200254235 | ISBN 9781774030981
  (softcover) | ISBN 9781774030998 (ebook)
Classification: LCC PS8601.T565 M37 2020 | DDC C811/.6—dc23

The Marta Poems

for Anthony and our girls
with much love

and for Marta

The Marta Poems

The Marta Poems

Testimonials

The Marta Poems take the reader on a compelling and lyrical narrative journey, through Marta's life and times as richly imagined by Susan J. Atkinson. She has wrought Marta's moving story with language so tenderly precise, you'll want to pause and savour each phrase, line and poem as the special treat it is before moving to the next. It's a 20th Century story with crisp imagery and lyric phrasing that will linger with the 21st Century reader for a long time to come. ~ *Rhonda Douglas, author of" Some Days I Think I Know Things: The Cassandra Poems".*

In Susan J. Atkinson's sure-footed debut collection, Marta, a displaced Polish girl, is shoved on a freight car bound for Siberia in 1941. A leather satchel, sewing kit and wedding photo acquire a talismanic importance in Marta's new refugee life. With psychic survival skills which include "pressing stars into a corner against the roof of her mouth," and real-world talents such as cutting squares of cloth from her slip to make embroidered hankies, Marta treks through a year as a slave laborer at a Soviet collective farm. Yet this is only the first stage of Marta's journey. She will have much to contend with as she moves from Rhodesia to England to Canada. Atkinson has an uncanny ability to place the reader in a freight car during a bread scuffle and then whisk them on to a sensual detail which Marta uses to ride out the ongoing squalor. Through a series of hauntingly memorable tableaus, this poet has taken one of history's buried victims and blown life into her story. ~ *Peter Richardson, author of "Sympathy for the Couriers".*

"*The Marta Poems* makes a tapestry of a life, with finely-stitched and intricate details. Marta's experiences span several continents and encompass moments of joy alongside deprivations both physical and emotional, as well as heart-breaking grief that "lingers on the clothesline". In telling Marta's story, Susan J. Atkinson pieces together fairy tales and war atrocities as expertly as Marta's own fine needlework, and always with immediacy and compassion." ~ *Frances Boyle, author of "This White Nest and Seeking Shade".*

The Marta Poems

Table of Contents

I Poland 1925-1941 ... 13

Marta — March 26th, 1925 ... 15
On Childhood ... 16
Father ... 17
Rapunzel, Rapunzel ... 18
On Loss ... 19
Stepmothers and Breadcrumbs ... 20
Beginning the Journey ... 22
Stepmothers and Apples ... 23
Namesday – July 27th, 1936 ... 24
Ladybird ... 25
Moving ... 26
September 7th, 1939 ... 27
Her Name – June 1940 ... 28

II Siberia 1941-1942 ... 29

June 12th, 1941 ... 31
This is How it Feels to be Alone ... 32
On the Way to Siberia ... 33
Bread ... 34
Onions ... 35
The Night Which Will Stay ... 36
Three Weeks Later ... 37
A Visit from Typhus and Dysentery ... 38
Sewing Skills ... 39
January 6th, 1942 ... 40
Pneumonia ... 41
Lucky at the Border — February 1942 ... 42

III Rhodesia 1942-1946 ... 43

Crossing the Caspian Sea ... 45
Daily Life ... 46
October 9th, 1945 ... 47
Afternoon Portrait ... 48

First Kiss ... 50
Rain ... 51
When Love Arrives ... 52
Lover, Beloved ... 53
February 15th, 1946 ... 55
Goodbye ... 56

IV England 1946-1948 ... 57

Leaving ... 59
April 23rd, 1946 ... 60
The Evening News ... 61
This is the Year ... 62
The Red House ... 63
March 1948 ... 64
The Morning After ... 65
Marta's Shadow ... 66
On Loneliness ... 67
Marta is Woken in the Night ... 68
Feeding the Ducks ... 70
Month Two ... 71
Wedding Day ... 72

V Canada 1949 – 2014 ... 73

Month Four ... 75
The Colour of Home ... 76
Sewing Roses ... 77
Month Nine ... 78
The Birth ... 79
After Irena's Birth ... 80
It is a Rare Occasion ... 81
Her Sunlight ... 83
Oh, How We Danced 84
John Takes Them to the Seaside ... 85
November ... 86
Lullaby ... 87
Waiting for the Coroner ... 88
When Ravens Cry ... 89

Grief ... 90
Changing the Clocks ... 91
Belly Aches ... 92
Stains Have Memories ... 93
The Weight of Such Things ... 94
What to do With All That Grief ... 95
Resting ... 96
Making Plans ... 97
In the Arboretum ... 98
Resolutions ... 99
Sewing Again ... 100
The Lightness of a Grackle ... 101
John Fades Away ... 102
All the Small Arguments ... 103
The Quiet Years ... 104
On Sleeping ... 105

Now ... 107

After Life ... 109

Acknowledgements ... 111
Notes ... 112

The Marta Poems

The Marta Poems

I
Poland
1925 - 1941

The Marta Poems

Marta – March 26th, 1925

She was born early

not quite ripe
arriving in the frozen air
serenaded by bashing winds
and bleating animals
sounds sung from hunger
and cold.

She was born early
torn from the mother's core
splitting a body in two

*(there are no other details
no one spoke of her birth).*

She didn't know the time,
whether it was light
dark or that curious colour
in between
when the sun settles in ribbons
and there's a quietness
before night –
she would have liked that.

On Childhood

Right from the beginning
she learned to make things up
and she learned how to sew –
patching pieces together
to make quilted blankets
soft and warm
just enough comfort
to swathe the guilt
of her mother's passing.

Of course the mother's death
wasn't really her fault,
the mother already
thinned by age
ripe with pleurisy –

simply gave up.

Marta learned
how to make elaborate
embroidered blankets –
squares styled from
the "Quilt of Belonging"
that did little good
when along came a stepmother
who had lived down their lane.

Father

Even as a young child Marta knows
her father is old, tired, perhaps
more grey than he should be.

He smells of coal and sweat.
His face darkened by soot,
cracked teeth white by contrast.

Marta barely knows
her father but tonight
after he has bathed

in the tub in the front room
he puts her on his feet and
jangles them both through a waltz.

He tells Marta tales at bedtime
of how she was born on a
Thursday and has far to go.

For now, she is here and he
is lonely and marries the nanny
who has cared for Marta since birth.

Rapunzel, Rapunzel

Marta wonders how
Rapunzel could stand
someone climbing
up her hair.
Every morning
her stepmother
pulls and tugs
clumps of curls
twisting strands
around the silver-
backed hairbrush.

Marta does not understand
why her stepmother
tears her hair
from its roots.
She does not understand
the green prickles
of envy that snag
youth in the teeth
of a matching comb.

On Loss

In this winter of frost lacing insides of windows
bitter cold sifts into small rooms on reedy sunlight.
Marta hears her father from his bed, constant cough
unfamiliar and guttural, she knows it's not good.

The doctor comes, the priest comes, no one talks
to Marta. The stepmother, *Macocha,* Anna,
as she has asked to be called, is rarely home.

Marta scuttles into her father's room
sideways like a crab as if that way
no one will see her. There is no one
to see her anyway. She devotes long hours
at her father's side, staring without touching.

She dares not touch. She has been taught,
washes her hands and rubs them raw.

Her father passes in the night.
A sudden quiet settles. His rattling breath
no longer punctures Marta's dreams.

By morning, his body has been taken.
Marta screams until she feels her throat will bleed
and the sobs will break her ribs.

Stepmothers and Breadcrumbs

I

Marta dreams of being left
in the woods where she can
walk alone, wander off the path
creep between dark shadows of
thick trunks perhaps stumble upon
a sweet cottage with gingerbread siding
and an old witch who would
take her in to fatten her up
with biscuits dipped in milky white tea

II

She dreams of featherbeds
soft down tickling cheeks
while she lazes
keeping fat
on thin bones
as meal after
delicious meal is served by
the crone with crooked fingers
curved toward a roaring fire

The Marta Poems

III

Marta dreams – stirs the fire
damp splinters
crackle insults
as she moves the pot
hands raw from cold
cinders on fingers
stepmother's breath
on her neck
no prince in sight

IV

She dreams of being
someone, anyone,
perhaps even
white-skinned-ruby-lipped
biting an apple or
sprinkling breadcrumbs on the path
heart cut open
by a woodsman.

Beginning the Journey

Marta is sent away
to a distant cousin
of her late father.

She travels by car,
her first car ride.

The new family have a bag
of peppermints to ward off
motion sickness.

Nervous and overwhelmed
Marta eats too many
and throws up over
shiny leather seats.

Stepmothers and Apples

Marta does not really believe her stepmother
will come looking for her, seeing as
she was all too willing to
parcel Marta to distant relatives
living in the country.

Her stepmother would not be likely to consult
a mirror on a wall, after all being fair meant bribing
a doctor-friend to give x-rays of a patient
with terminal tuberculosis so that when she
coughed into the handkerchief pressed to her lips
she secured an audience with a Gestapo head,
who stood a good distance proving a familiar paranoia
of virus and bacteria was alive and well
without much of a do all she had to do
was whisper she was to undergo a cure in Switzerland
her passport stamped - off she went.

No, it's not likely but even so
in the little cottage in the woods
with a family that treat her
like a princess, Marta
is wary of apples
especially the red ones.

Namesday – July 27th, 1936

In this house
that cares about

things, Marta wakes
to the scent of

blue cornflowers
alstroemeria and

bright blooms
with freckled petals.

A chair waits
at the foot of

the table decorated in
celebration of this day.

There are small gifts
scattered around.

At her place
a braided crown of

chamomiles and poppies
atop a leather-bound diary.

Ladybird

Ladybird, Ladybird fly away home
your house is on fire and

everything is gone
the house burned

to bare bones
its skeleton a rack of

charred wood
a few tatters of colour

caught by blackened nails
struggling madly to be free.

Marta recognizes scraps from
her Sunday Best, tries to reach them

grasps too hard and a beam
crashes creating new sparks.

Clutching a brown leather satchel
she runs to safety in the middle of the lawn.

Moving

The family loses everything that was in the house.
Lucky for Marta she has her diary and satchel
and is wearing her favourite dress.
The family still has their gold and

candlesticks that were hidden in the hay-bales
in the stable behind the house. Wrapped in old coats
the family carries them to the neighbouring cottage

where they will all live for the time being.
The matron is sour-looking
with greasy hair and blank brown eyes,
she invites them into her home, feeds the family

makes beds in the small cramped space.
Marta gulps at the bowl of soup,
blobs of beaten egg white floating on top –
boats navigating grey waters.

September 7th, 1939

*All everyone can talk about is the war
and a man called Adolf Hitler.
Uncle says Hitler and his German army
have crashed across our Polish borders
and that they were lucky to have good weather.*

The grown-ups are calling it Blitzkrieg - Lightning War.

*It's all over the news how the Germans
bombed railroads and highways
smashing my beloved Warsaw in a surprise attack.*

*Uncle says we're too young to listen to the radio,
but we hide behind the door and listen anyway.
The report I heard was how thousands tried to flee.
Main roads overflowed with people, their belongings
pulled in carts or carried, heavy on weakened shoulders.*

*The radio said everybody on the road to Bzezing
was machine-gunned down by low-flying German aircrafts,
the road left clogged with the corpses of people and horses.*

*Everyone says we are safe here. We are busy bees
as crops of wheat and potatoes
are harvested and hidden in storage.*

*One of our neighbours has organized us into groups.
We can gather white moss from the bottom of Lake Zielone
so it may be dried to use for antiseptic dressings.*

Uncle says we must do our part.

Her Name – June 1940

Marta practices writing her name
plays at adding an h.

These days there's a lot of
talk about names

how they sound, how they look
what hints they may give.

Marta doesn't think she needs the h
though she can't be sure,

besides, she's only playing and
surely no one will say anything.

Still, she is careful to be alone
as she circles the loop of ink

a murmur on the paper
through the straight line

stiff back of the letter
supporting the bend of the bridge

a perfect h, perfectly spaced
between the t and the a

joining both letters as if it belonged
in case it is needed.

The Marta Poems

**II
Siberia
1941 - 1942**

The Marta Poems

The Marta Poems

June 12th, 1941

*We have been arrested. For what I don't know
but officers have searched our home and
we were instructed to each pack a bag.*

*I have my warmest boots and coat – Aunt Patrycja
said we will need them, and I have my diary,
my leather satchel and my sewing kit.*

*We piled into an open truck with so many others-
similar trucks parked outside our neighbours.
We were not the only ones.*

*Not until we arrive in the small town with
a large railway junction do I experience the worst.*

*The open truck drove up to a long cattle car
and we were told to climb in with our belongings.
I tripped and dropped my satchel, everything fell
and I scrambled to put it all back together
but when I looked up everyone had been pushed ahead,
devoured by the crowds and I was left alone
blown from side to side on the platform until I was lifted
and thrown into the next available car.*

This is How it Feels to be Alone

Marta weeps.
She is alone

the family divided
on the crowded platform.

She prays for their safety.
She prays for her own.

Buries her head
stuffs her fist in her mouth

blocking the shriek
that threatens to bubble

and burst from the base
of her throat.

The Marta Poems

On the Way to Siberia

Tongue slack with thirst,
bare boards cold through thin clothes.

Marta is lost between the seasons, somewhere
across the border into Russia. In the distance dark soil lies

like a sheet spotted here and there with purple dots;
abandoned beetroot— no one left to collect them.

She rattles Eastward with the bones of ghosts, lolls
in the overcrowded stench of the railcar wagon.

Trapped in closeness, others' kneecaps like sharp sticks
poking her thighs. Someone tosses moldy bread
onto the floor; everyone scrambles like hogs at a trough,

except the woman with young children
who slumps silent and numb. Marta can't stand it,

pretends to admire the view from the tiny slats –
snapshots of pine forests without the scent.

No sign of life. She tucks herself
into a parcel of air, no bigger than a leaf,

bends her body into the curl of a caterpillar,
praying summer will bring fresh air and wings.

Bread

The man thinks he is being kind
when he tosses the bread to land
somewhere in the middle of the cattle car.
Moldy puffs cloud the air
breaking into bits
    as women and children scratch
    the bare wood floor,
    hens pecking for corn,
    green fluff sticking
    to out-stretched tongues
    dry as bone.

Marta stares horrified
her pride presses
to the bench
hands grasping
raw wood
a scream crawling
from the back
of her throat
along the inside
of her mouth
loses steam
and gasps

    from the 'o'
    of her blistered lips.

Onions

Cooped with others
in cattle cars
no idea of destination
Marta licks cracked lips

jagged like broken
Christmas ornaments, dry shards
stabbing her tongue
hanging like a dog
panting desperate for water
the train stops at a station

after days of travel
wailing and howling
swelling around her
Marta guzzles the boiler water
siphoned into pots
the liquid scorching
into blisters and sores

she does not care
she sees the soldier
smells the odor

a bucketful of white onions perfect globes
skin so thin she can taste their heart

ripped lips swollen raw pucker
sucking hunger she takes his stare

promising to do anything.

The Night Which Will Stay

his taste
lasted for days
she sucked
her fingers
peeling skin raw
just to remember

and she did
remember
peeling clothes
like layers
of an onion
thin scraps
covering thin
flesh burying
hidden
sweetness.

Three Weeks Later

It has been roughly three weeks of travel
but Marta survives the journey.

She arrives at the third stop and for a third time
three wagons are uncoupled, hers is one of them.

Again, she is pushed toward an open truck.
No sign of family who may have continued east.

Marta travels through grasslands – the Altai Mountains
growing into dark peaks in the far distance.

Wooden barracks and small huts poke out of
the tall grasses, temporary homes waiting

for assignment. Marta is fortunate to find herself
in one of the log cabins that has a little insulation.

There is no time to settle, work begins the next day.
Marta toils through fields and fields of wheat,

pulls out all the thistle, returns late in the evenings, hands
blistered and bleeding, prickles digging under her skin.

Marta loses weight. There is so little to eat and she is
almost out of goods to barter for food. She is given

bread and is glad of the wild strawberries she finds
in the hedgerows. The children in the barracks fish

along the banks of the River Sosra. Marta happily donates
her hairpins to make hooks so she may at least have a taste of fish soup.

A Visit from Typhus and Dysentery

Arriving with an angry stomach
wanting to be heard

it grumbles and hisses in anger
eager to spit out the poison that

has spread quickly from something
as every-day and simple as salted fish.

Hollow insides hug ribs
with every convulsion.

She is afraid to breathe
as heat coils its tongue

and yanks at
empty guts.

Heave after heave
everything comes up.

Marta fades to black
a swarm of bees mingle

behind shut eyes.

Sewing Skills

Summer unwinds and the supply of goods
worth bartering diminishes into barren air.

Marta's agile fingers itch to sew as she slowly
rips material from her cotton slip, shortening

her hemline ever so slightly. From this length of fabric
she cuts squares and with the last of her fine thread

crochets a delicate border. She makes five
pocket handkerchiefs to sell at Sunday market.

The next week she does the same.
As her slip noticeably shortens

so do the days. Fall is fast approaching and
she needs to work nights to harvest the grain.

The Germans continue to advance. In the distance
dark mountains are the only promise of escape.

January 6th, 1942

A miracle. Everyone is whispering
news – an amnesty for Poles.
We will be issued identity papers.
We will be named allies, which means
once again, we will board a train.

Months of waiting a truck arrives
to take everyone back to the station.

We huddle against the night
-30c, temperatures still plummeting

everything frozen but hope
until arriving at the station

hundreds already there
we will not be leaving tonight.

Our comfort – a full moon glistening
over the shore of a large lake.

Pneumonia

Perhaps from that frozen night
perhaps from months of starvation

her fever boils at 42 degrees
in the makeshift hospital

delirious her frozen bones
shiver to stay warm

fire prickles at the surface
of her paper-thin skin.

The fevered ghost of
her recent illness

re-ignites and
burns through her body.

Lucky at the Border – February 1942

Marta is at a makeshift hospital
beside the train station

sleep brings darkness and the half-
whispers of those around her.

Watery rice soup and salted fish
the carrier of poison

has spread like a bruise
through her body.

She is lucky to have made it here
to survive the night

she has seen the sunken eyes and taut
flesh over bones that the dead wear.

She is lucky, a nurse changes
her dirty sheets

she shivers to stay warm
everything loosens, too weak

to feel any embarrassment, Marta
does not notice her own stench

her only fear, that her journey will end –
another ghost by the train tracks.

The Marta Poems

**III
Rhodesia
1942 - 1946**

The Marta Poems

Crossing the Caspian Sea

Marta travels by filthy transport overflowing with
human freight to Krasnovodsk at the shores of the sea.

Immune, she shrugs at these scenes, the weak unable
to make a final voyage, dying with freedom in sight.

The trip lasts two full days. The boat batted between
surging waves and strong winds blowing from the north.

Marta spends the journey with one arm wrapped around
the railing the other around her diary and leather satchel.

She is too ill to be sea-sick, watches waves bow and bend
into fantastical creatures and imaginary lands.

Arriving in Persia she is stripped of louse-ridden rags
and issued new clothes. She sips on soup, pushing aside

chunks of lamb. There is plenty to eat and passengers gorge
but for Marta painful memories of dysentery still haunt.

She will wait until they arrive in Rhodesia,
there is still a long way to go.

Daily Life

Marta soon becomes accustomed to life at camp.
She volunteers for three hours each day, helps

cook and clean to keep the communal areas in
good order. She learns bananas are the cheapest fruit,

how to catch birds with a sling shot, how to avoid
troops of monkeys and baboons.

The area is fertile enough to plant small farms
pineapples, maize, tomatoes and rows of golden sunflowers.

In the evenings, the women gather in the community center
sewing clothes from bolts of fabric given to the camp.

Sometimes Marta does not go. She wants to be alone
to listen to crickets singing above the voices of the women.

Her round hut smells of damp mud and in the night
the shutter latch clicks and clacks like a runaway train.

The sounds cut her sleep but there are no lights,
no electricity. Marta lies in the dark wondering

if this is how insomnia starts. Dreams raw from war, starvation
and loss. She keens for pink to rise through the open window.

The Marta Poems

October 9th, 1945

*Life has been quiet and routine
for over three and a half years
but now I am filled with an emotion
I have never felt before – a longing.
When I turned my face up
towards him, his dark eyes
looked down at me and I saw
his matching desire pulsing
in the brightness of his eyes.
We both know it is wrong,
that whatever we are feeling
we must stop but perhaps
there is no harm for now.*

*I suspect the greater danger is in
the trade. We have been given bolts of
white and grey linen, which myself and two
others in the camp are using to sew dresses.
We also have cotton and embroidery thread
and I have made some simple patterns, easy to follow.
We have found a way to sell the clothes to local people –
my new friend is helping. We will have to be careful.*

*I am trying not to make things complicated but
tomorrow night he has invited me to the cinema in town.
I have only been out of the camp a few times
but I have seen the cinema and oh how
I would love to go to the pictures. There is a new film
that some of the women are talking about –
A Tree Grows in Brooklyn, I think it is called.
It sounds good.*

The Marta Poems

Afternoon Portrait

I

dressed in plain grey,
head scarf around neck
apron loose, hair braided,
Marta waits on the corner

one barefoot kicks the dry dirt
at the curb.

Her yellow boot in hand, she stares
at the inside

fishes out a pebble the size of a pea
that has rubbed her sole raw.

II

She is caught in the rain
hopscotches to avoid puddles

shelters in a doorway
until the worst passes

all that's left of the storm
are clouds of wet wool

lying low in the dark sky

still she waits across the road
until, in another doorway
she sees him, waves, and
he leaps over the streaming water.

III

in a doorway

where the rain
has punched the

muddy edges
of the curb

where nothing
will grow

he brings
her into

the circle of
his arms and

kisses her for
the first time.

First Kiss

The kiss he sipped
when he pressed
his lips

to each
of her fingertips

was so soft and sweet

like a tame bird
pecking at seed

and when he finally
pressed his lips
to hers

hundreds of roses
exploded in her mouth.

Rain

January brings the heaviest of rains
Marta knows she would surely
have drowned in the torrential downpours
if not for this new-found love that keeps her afloat.

She can't wait for work to be finished
for the storms to shelter their meetings
for the drops that are so round and big
to splash into the puddles like pearls.

Every afternoon the rains cascade
adding to the humidity, heating
the skies and the ground, so that
everything drips, even when the air clears

all that is left is the snarl of clouds
the rain quietly clicking in the trees.

When Love Arrives

after a series of rather unfortunate relationships,
it comes so well disguised she almost does not recognize it.

It pushes in from the sea, heady summer wind,
storm brewing
at first indistinguishable from the gushing heat
of a one-night stand.

It teases like rain in August,
the kind that spits polka dots,
the kind one wouldn't know whether to trust,
not knowing if it's enough to quench

after a long drought, but when it pours,
drenching beneath her skin,
Marta prays it will last and stretches her tongue
to catch every drip.

The Marta Poems

Lover, Beloved
(after "The Perfect Poem" Heather McHugh)

Being both a lover and beloved is new for her,
for Marta who has travelled
far from her home and
the lost family, who took care of her
when no one else cared.

Now here she is in a small white doorway
discovering the truth about love.
She is waiting for her new-found lover,
a man with sweet cinnamon skin
who may be forbidden

but she cannot resist and as
angels lie in sun
Marta will become a lover and
will become beloved.

In a small white doorway
sheltered from the monsoon rain
falling in angry blisters, steam rising
from the streams of water
Marta waits.

She has been in Rhodesia for three years,
the heat unbearable, the rains intolerable
but she has a place to stay
away from the bombs,
away from starvation,
away from everything she has known

and now she has fallen into temptation.
Like a boat bends towards sea
her body bends towards his,
her back arched away from
the soft splinters of palm leaf fronds,
the cotton of her summer dress flowing

around them, the fingers of his right hand,
light on the circle of her small fabric buttons,
his other arm curled around her waist,
her face upturned, lips swollen and ripe,
as he lowers for another kiss.

February 15th, 1946

*We have all been warned about our relationships.
Evacuees are no longer allowed to be friends
with Africans. We are to keep to ourselves.
Gone will be the days where locals teach us
how to eat grasshoppers and how to pick and eat
the fruits as their juices ripen.*

*There have been too many complaints about Poles
trespassing outside the camp, fishing, swimming
and causing nuisance at the lake fishing area.
Everything will be out of bounds. We have been called
an influence on society, which needs to stop. Even worse
a letter has been issued about African involvement with us.*

*Africans have been warned about purchasing
anything that we make, especially the garments
we have sewn from the goods given to the camp.
My man and I both know this; we have been told
and know that one day soon we may be caught.
Neither of us could stand this.*

*And now there is talk of how there was never an intention
to keep myself and the other evacuees in South Africa –
it was temporary, perhaps it is time to leave.
What is most sad is knowing my dream of returning
to a free country has died. I cannot resign to Stalinist rule
I must consider following the rumours
and look at maybe settling in England.*

*P.s. and to think yesterday was Valentines
and we were so happy.
We ate smuggled chocolate
and shared a bottle of maize-beer.*

Goodbye

They pretend it is not.
Look at the moon he tells her,
look for it and I will too.

Tonight, they watch the moon.
Wisps of clouds fringe its edges –
eyelashes on a half-closed eye.

Darkness needs no sound.
Swallowing quiet
Marta turns and leaves.

**IV
England
1946 - 1948**

The Marta Poems

Leaving

The wind tastes like March
a word
chews at the tip
of Marta's tongue
biting a hole for the
wind to whistle through.
It makes a sound like a name
from long ago
familiar yet distant
and Marta can't quite
catch it.

She is on a boat
on the way
to England
the wind
carries everything
she's ever known
into the salt-licked air.

April 23rd, 1946

*The smash of the waves in open sea is replaced by clickety-clack
of the rails as I travel North from London to Yorkshire.
The ship passage was quite unremarkable
except for the joyful serenade from our Italian crew.*

*In my carriage I have met a young man with his bicycle.
He tells me about riding through this country, his country –
from John O'Groats to Land's End.*

*During our journey train tracks divide the fields
parting waves of green as we rush through.*

*Frank, the young Englishman, tells me about a recent trip he took
to the Scottish Highlands. How he was buffeted by rain
and a bullying wind that pushed his bicycle over rough roads
and desolate stretches of nothing.*

*He was enthralled by the ghostly shapes looming behind the muffled fog
despite his orange cycling cape ripping at the buttonholes from his neck
to his knees leaving the garment to flap madly around his drenched body.*

*He tells me he saw the most unusual sight.
Waves lapping over green fields,
the sea on land, trees growing almost at water's edge
and thousands of shells all colours and sizes
scattered on the side of the road.*

*It was the most delightful train ride I have experienced.
Frank says I really must go and see Ben Loyal while I am here.
He says it is a mountain of majestic proportions.*

The Evening News
(May 11, 1946)

In the guest house the table
is ready, napkins and cutlery

shine at each setting,
the dining room will be full tonight.

Thick slabs of granary bread
curls of butter

wait for the guests huddled
around the radio,

their own stories of the day
quieted as they

listen to the news.
Sixty-one SS members

from Mauthausen
concentration camp, Dachau,

were convicted of murdering
seventy thousand people.

Someone clicks the radio off,
the guests gather at the table.

Marta waits at the window – and wonders
what can possibly hold the moon in the sky?

This is the Year

Twenty-one and Marta
will taste Brussel sprouts
for the first time.

She will go to the pictures
will paint lines
with a fine brush
dipped in gravy browning
down the back of her legs.

Raspberry red
will stain her lips
and stiletto heels tip-
tap all night as she
dances to every song.

She will laugh out loud
without fear of being caught
and will believe in England
where the slightest of breezes

suggest life may get better.

The Red House

At the bedsit
Marta meets
a beautiful, young girl
with wide blue eyes
who dreams of being in the movies.

The young actress knows of a place
where other actors meet to talk
of the world and politics.

The house is cradled in the heart
of the pastoral mid-North,
where stone divides green.

The young actress wonders if Marta
might like to do some sewing.
Perhaps make patches and arm bands
from scraps of red.

Marta notices gold thread
poking out from the actress's handbag.

That night a chain of stars
chases Marta in her dreams.
She stirs feeling a slight pull
like a necklace pinching.

March 1948

The mold of the moors
sits on Marta's chest
scratches like wool on
the inside of her skin.

The air is too fresh,
too damp, bracken and moss
cling to her lungs
grey wheezes in her breath.

Gossip spreads Polish
displaced refugees are
leaving for a new world
sailing to Canada.

Marta spends hours doing her hair
smudging lipstick on lips and cheeks
pinking her smile
ready for the camera.

She sends the tiny photograph
to an address given by a friend.

Marta hears nothing back.

The Marta Poems

The Morning After

Looking back on the night before when she'd pressed
the stars into a corner against the roof of her mouth
Marta wondered if she'd perhaps made a mistake.
She hadn't meant to go home with the Polish soldier
with hollow eyes but she'd been lonely,
longing for the taste of her homeland
with its earthy roots of purple beets and dirty white potatoes.
She had other excuses too.

It never rained on Saturdays but earlier that day grey
smothered the town drowning her Polish optimism
and she was missing the man with sweet cinnamon skin.
Long and the short of it she'd done all kinds of things
she wouldn't normally do.

She'd guzzled straight shots of vodka, swayed to the swing of music,
flirted with the soldiers, played the sultry vixen and finally
she'd swaggered upstairs to lie with the soldier whose hollow eyes
hadn't really seen her as he'd fumbled with her brassiere fastener
and her undergarments without unhooking her stockings.

It was over quickly. No bombs had fallen in heady explosion,
no angels had sung in serenade, the stars lay still
as a familiar blanket of disappointment covered her half naked body.

The soldier had scuttled away and locked himself in the tiny bathroom,
his low whimpers pushing through the silence,
his anguish gathering in speed like a runaway train chugging
into a high-pitched squeal.

She hadn't waited.

Sucking on the stars that hadn't moved
and were still pressed into a corner
against the roof of her mouth,
Marta walked ramrod straight all the way home.

Marta's Shadow

wears red sequins
long tight dresses
stiletto heels
leaves no footprints
sneaks
out after dark
prowls like a stray cat
comes home muddy
and tired
the moon a silver scythe
in her eye
stars sweetening her breath

Marta's shadow would never have done what Marta did,
wouldn't have stayed with the nervous soldier
holding his shrieking head night after night.

Not Marta's shadow.
She'd drown
a man lost at sea
rather than curl
her arms to save him.

On Loneliness

Loneliness seeps into pores
sinks into veins, falls into the cracks
where disappointments loiter
with all those that came before

Marta finds herself returning
into the stiff arms of the haunted soldier
whose own shyness
gives strange comfort

but loneliness hovers in
the crumpled bedsheets
which cool too quickly
thinness of need
scent of emptiness
crouching in the hollow bedsit

she smells it in her clothes
her hair
her skin

Marta leaves in the milky air of morning
loneliness following in the shadows,
biting at her heels, each bite a reminder
that she will return the next night and the next.

Marta is Woken in the Night

by a butter knife prying her eyes,
sharpness of the moon slitting her sleep

I

a craving startles her
room exhaling the scent of onions
and suddenly Marta wants one
wants to peel its gossamer layers
scrape the threads through her teeth
just to taste the memory of
the Russian soldier

II

these forbidden lusts waken her fully
desperate to pee
she creeps downstairs
an unfamiliar buzzing
an unknown stirring
vibrating close to her core

III

in the cupboard beside the sink
a basket of yellow onions
quietly ages, wrinkled skin
falling like the browned pages of a book
Marta unfurls the first unblemished layer
bites into the ball
ripe and round

The Marta Poems

IV

acid pinches her cheeks
and she tastes the Russian soldier
bitter shame spreading
in her mouth, down her throat
into her stomach
where vile heat pushes its way up

V

Marta hangs over the sink
memories, onions, sickness swelling
until it's too much
and it all comes up
leaving only
the unfamiliar stirring
beating its wings

VI

in the bedroom upstairs across the hall
from her own room
John paces in his sleep
a dog chasing rabbits
dropping between dreams

VII

she hears him keening but stays downstairs
spiraled on the front mat
squashed against the door
she waits like a package
to be picked up and taken away.

Feeding the Ducks

Sun lightens the weight of the moors from Marta's chest
its straw-thin rays burning through scorched skies –
the hottest Autumn in fifty years
where the leaves cling to branches,
reddened edges curling and crisp, refusing to fall.

She and John walk through the public gardens,
down by the pond, quiet, companionable.

A child, no older than four dangles over the stone edging,
her mother clutches her coat tail
as the child throws chunks of bread
at the madly quacking ducks.

Squinting in afternoon light,
Marta mistakes the grey of the path
for the floor of a railcar, 1941 Siberia
and a family of children beyond hunger, mewl like kittens
as they suck on dry bread, too weak to bite.

She feels the strange stirring, turns, throws up a breakfast
of porridge, kippers and powdered eggs.
John catches her, sits her on a park bench, she slumps
against his shoulder, wipes her mouth
with the checkered handkerchief from his pocket.

John's free hand picks up something from the ground –
a thumbnail photograph. He smooths the creases.
A flattened face peeps out.
Marta recognizes the stretched smile from months ago.
John asks her to move away with him.
She throws up again, but it is decided.

Month Two

Marta smooths
the round pebble
of her belly
she's starting to show
and gossip spits
at the walls of the house
cold and mean like November rain

Marta sits on the porch
covers her ears to the nosy wrens
chirping over the fence
the sparrows pecking
at her tightening clothes

she knows what they're saying
and now even the leggy tulips
are joining in
losing their balance
bending close to one another
fleshy heads whispering
"did you hear…oh the scandal…
trapped him you know…"

Marta wishes they were right
the twittering a melody
compared to John screaming
in his sleep.

Marta smooths the round
pebble of her belly
truth is she knows
who trapped who.

Wedding Day

Marta wears a twill suit
in the darkest shade of grey
with every movement
cream speckles shiver
in the light
tricking the eye.

The collar of her jacket
is pearlized and matches
her shoes, which barely fit.
Her feet swollen and sore
from the pregnancy
spill over the sides of
her dainty footwear.

A court photographer
snaps a quick shot
sends it weeks later
Marta makes space
on the mantlepiece
presses a petal from
her bouquet, sticking it
against the picture's
flimsy backing.

The Marta Poems

**V
Canada
1949 - 2014**

The Marta Poems

Month Four

Marta squeals the first time
fists punch her bulging belly.
Through pale skin she touches

the unborn child, strokes the tiny frame,
follows the road map of stretch marks
just beginning to bruise

along the sides of her stomach.
John is sitting in his chair,
the green one, under the window.

A spot of light colours his hair
Marta notices a few grey strands
threading through the brown.

Tenderness dances between them
as she crosses the room
takes John's hand rests it

on her bareness. The baby wakes to
his touch, rolls as if on waves.
Marta giggles with each movement,

they guess at body parts as the baby
sprawls and settles. The light outside
dimming around them.

The Colour of Home

New home, in a new country,
Marta's books and sewing patterns furnish bare rooms.
The house is small and attached on one side,
but theirs, none-the-less, and Marta is hopeful
in her new home, in her new country their family will grow.

The street is quiet, young trees line its sides,
ash and linden with small leaves that offer music
in the gentle mornings as a cardinal hops from twig
to grape vine, red darting between leaves.

Marta spends these early hours in the garden,
alyssum hems the front and small yellow flowers
polka dot the lawn reminding her of the golden glow
of childhood buttercups under her chin.

Now in her own home she will have everything. She will bake
decadent desserts with creamy butter and dark brown sugar.
She will sew lace curtains with delicate scalloped edges
to blow breezily at the small front window,
and in the back where the southern exposure catches
afternoon sun, she will grow vegetables and fruit.
Perhaps by the fence a strawberry patch, from which
she will pick only the ripest red to make jams and pies.

There will be cucumbers to pickle and put up in the cold
cellar beside the beets that stain the kitchen counter
as she cuts into deep purple flesh reminding her when
home was narrow fields and meadows coloured with warm ocher

wheat and rye and the fresh green of potato plants, all abandoned
in the home she had fled years and years before.

Sewing Roses

Marta's neighbor tells her of an old wives' tale she's heard;
a wishful way to determine the sex of her unborn child.

The neighbor holds a needle high above Marta's left palm,
steadying the sharp silver point dangling from a length of thread.

Inside Marta's womb the new life wriggles and worms
rolling in time to the needle set free to dance across her skin.

In the furrows of her open hand, the slender shaft sews tiny patterns
carving circled petals; the rose ready to bloom will be a girl.

Month Nine

Marta wakes ready and round
a full moon bursting.

In the heat of an early summer morning
an urge to walk pushes her outside.

Marta plucks wildflowers down by the river
heady-scented blooms to decorate the crib of her unborn child.

In her small sanctuary of books
she has read of the boy who named flowers,

his wooden cradle laced with vines, *phlox and hemerocallis*
his gift of naming borne through this smallest of touches.

Marta hopes to bring such greatness to the child
swelling in her core.

She thinks of the baby boy dreaming his names,
Rosa and Alyssum
dusky nectar sweetening his breath
forming classifications of flora.

Ambling home, her drooping hem
catching on the dew-dampened grass

reminding her of the pile of sewing she has let grow,
for once she has not tried to fix things.

In the afternoon, a young girl
whom Marta does not yet know will slip into her dreams
long hair flowing, flowers dripping from hands,
smile curving like a slivered crescent.

The Birth

Marta is beached
on the couch
(the one with the tiny flowered print)
she is wet with sweat and the couch
bows like a horse's back
sagging from weight and age.

It is time
everything sweats under this June sun
outside birds melt on wires
squashed from heat like plump raisins
their incessant gossip greeting *the położna* who comes
to the house with a small doctor's bag in hand.

The położna hopes the birth will not be difficult –
there will be no one else to attend.
When she arrives, Marta is stranded on the couch
the whirring of the birds driving her near-mad
the położna knows what to do, guides Marta upstairs, brings tubs
of steaming water and piles of clean towels.

It is time
John arrives home and *the położna* snaps orders at his bent head
banishes him to the short hall outside the room
nervous and fidgety he paces until it's all too much.

He leans against the door feels soft mud,
slams his eyes shut, hands slapped against ears,
slapped against the muffled voices,
the crying, the screaming, the whirring of the birds.

Walls shrink into a narrow trench
a distant glow flares through his clenched eyes
John sinks beside the closed door.

Through the harrowing night
he lies arched and still.

After Irena's Birth

Marta wakes in the night
a warm wetness blushes between
her legs, her womb sighs
tightens and grips, but the blood
comes and won't stop.

Fear of waking John and Irena
stifles her desire to scream
but the wetness spreading
on the bedding stirs John.

Marta can't hang on
drifts into black and wakes
to find herself tucked
and hemmed into a hospital bed
with crisp white sheets.

She is mesmerized
by the one slack-skinned arm
that lies outside the cocoon
its tubes, like worms
poking into her pale blue veins.

A doctor visits,
explains what has happened
the need to operate
the D and C
I'm sorry there will be no more children.

Beside Marta's bed,
Irena in her crib,
sucks the air looking for milk
Marta smiles, they have a beautiful daughter
it is enough.

It is a Rare Occasion

When John's boss and his wife come to visit
with their four daughters, who coo
and sing lullabies to baby Irena before dinner.

Marta has prepared a feast of Perogies
and cabbage rolls. Borscht made with
fresh beets from the garden.

Marta wins over the children
with smiles and compliments.
At the table she teaches the youngest girl

how to fold napkins into beautiful things.
Her slim nimble fingers
bend the stiff fabric into pleats

molding colour, manipulating folds
until she has made a baby's cradle,
a rose, a swan, all symbols of love,

skillfully modelled from the frigid damask.
Marta slips shy glances at John
hoping to catch his approval.

She answers questions in a gentle voice
so the table strains to hear and
she snatches everyone's attention

like the wind snatching
at the fine linens that will
later blow on the clothesline.

Throughout dinner Marta relaxes
smiles proudly, chest puffed
as the sculptures pile up.

The Marta Poems

Each of the daughters
passes her napkin wanting more.
Everyone is engaged, completely absorbed

until John spills his glass,
burgundy blushing wide
across the tablecloth and

the attention snaps
as the girls rush to drop their napkins
bandaging the damage

the swans, the roses,
the crib undone,
stained red, deep as blood.

Her Sunlight

Marta enjoys the quiet of the morning,
watches Irena plant her foot in a pool of sunshine,

shadow of her tiny body fluttering through warmth
like a butterfly ready to land

the child is mesmerized by the falling petals of light
bends to smell them, touch them, pick them

feet taste the custard pool, shadow eating sunlight
until it has gone, and she crawls along the floor

sinks so close to the ground, face pressed body curled
around the buttery yellow splashes, a comma at the end

of an unfinished poem,

Oh, How We Danced

Marta is tired but happy
Irena has brought light into John's eyes

life into his bones.
Marta has not been able to settle the child

but John cradles the tiny swaddle
and waltzes around

the small sitting room
Irena's eyelids drop

she sleeps peacefully
safe in the nest of his arms.

The Marta Poems

John Takes Them to the Seaside

to the closest coastline
where the Atlantic laps
the shore in cold folds.

They go for a long weekend
and stay in a quaint hotel
along the seafront.

In the afternoon
they walk by the shore
paddle in the shallows.
John's pant legs rolled to the knees
Marta's skirts tucked and tied
around her thighs.

They take turns carrying Irena.
John swings her small body
over the waves.
Marta sculpts a sandcastle
the red sand sticking
beneath her nails.
She builds four towers
with walls connecting each,
finds shells to decorate.

She sits Irena in the middle
and John knots the corners
of his striped handkerchief,

bows low as he crowns
his young daughter
Queen of the Castle.

It is August
Irena is one.

November

November was the month when everything
in the house burned hotter than summer.

Inside the walls on fire with a heaving fever
sharp needles prickling the sour sick air.

Outside the wind mewled long and forlorn and
the ghost began its rattling in the little girl's chest.

Marta knows her child and knows
she is too quiet, too stiff, too still.

By afternoon, the child's shadow is at its longest
brittle against Marta's fresh-washed sheets.

Marta sees the flames of sickness swallowing
her child and she knows it won't be long.

The girl burns, the wind screams and Marta pinches
tiny shards of aspirin through tight lips.

Within hours the girl's skin is blushed-blue, mouth coated powder-white
body numb as cheeks slapped ruby by mid-autumn wind.

November was the month when everything
in the house burned hotter than summer.

Lullaby

Marta spends hours in Irena's nursery
her small daughter on her lap.

She drips water from a teaspoon into
the little girl's mouth, holds her chest

to ear to hear the patter of her heart.
Marta haunts the nursery, prays the fever will break.

In the night she watches Irena sleep.
In the morning she scoops her

from the crib to her arms and rocks
her in the chair through the quiet hours.

Irena sleeps curled like a kitten
on her lap and Marta hums

lullaby after lullaby. By mid-afternoon
thin streaks of light catch dust

and Marta stops singing. She, too is cradled
in the warmth of the room and drowses.

When she wakes her head is tilted close to Irena's chest
to listen for the flutter of her heart.

Marta puts her cheek to her daughter's nose feels
for the slip of warm breath from her mouth.

But there is nothing. The room is so still Marta catches
her own breath to stop the pounding in her ears.

Waiting for the Coroner

In the cold room where jars of pickles
and sweet preserves stand in line,
neatly labelled and perfectly uniform
on the freshly-papered shelves,
Marta waits.

In the dining room, Irena is laid out,
tiny and pale against the blistered
wood of the oak table.

John, unable to stand the quiet
is at the bottom of the garden
in the small garage against the fence
rocking with grief.

Marta waits alone in the cold room.

When Ravens Cry

Marta wakes when the ravens cry
and settle in the branches of the maple
in front of the house.
For a moment, the cries sound like Irena
but it can't be.

In the echo of midnight
Marta remembers her daughter is gone.

She remembers it all –
the sinking November sun
closing the day
her child curved around the faded
cotton pillow clutching its softness
as she slipped like the sunlight
behind the swaying spruces
until she was gone.

Marta wakes to the cry of ravens
and cannot fall back to sleep.

She crawls from bed to door
stands in the yard, still as stone
as snowflakes fall dressing her shivering body
clothing her bare arms in white.

In the maple tree the ravens quiet themselves
black spots on white-covered branches

and Marta waits
for the chill to creep into her bones.

Grief

hides in her drawer between
folded socks and underwear,

weaves into cotton and flannel,
breathable materials that let it live and heave.

Marta scrubs at every corner
washes everything twice, thrice,

over and over but grief
lingers on the clothesline clinging

to the pegs and the legs
of small sleepers never worn but waiting

for the child to grow a few sizes,
for her limbs to curve into their softness.

Marta senses rain, checks from the door,
thinks she sees something in the corner of her eye,

afternoon sun blinks and it looks like a child
walking across the line, a tight-rope walker confident and sure.

But she's wrong. There's no sign of rain, no clouds, no child,
just a shadow, heavy and grey, holding hands with grief.

Changing the Clocks

Marta refuses
to change the clocks

to set them back
and make

one more hour
of darkness

instead she lives
in limbo

one hour that
doesn't fit

lingers and
balances

as blue turns
to grey

turns to black.

Belly Aches

It has been a year since
Irena's passing and still
the dark pit of sorrow ferments.

Her doctor has tried
treatment after treatment
yet Marta does the unthinkable

and visits a naturopath
who tells her she will get
these pangs from time to time.

Aches not from her stomach
but from her heart.

Stains Have Memories

Marta has heard somewhere
how stains remember
   their smell   their colour
she weeps at the sight
of Irena's room
cleaned so many times
it can't be possible
for a stain to remain
to remember all the things
she wishes it could.

All these years
memories slipping from bones
sweet-milk-scent gone
   the weight of the child
in her arms now empty
      the tug on her breast
late in the night forgotten.

She cannot forgive herself for
scrubbing away the stain
   the feel   the smell.

On hands and knees
Marta digs like a dog
searching for a bone
rips up green fibers
clumps like grass
sticking beneath her bleeding nails
that drip a new stain
on the carpet in Irena's room.

The Weight of Such Things

Marta still bakes with precision
    puts up rows and rows
        of pickles and jams
            neat and orderly
                in the cold room

she still cooks and bakes
    but no longer measures

when measured, everything feels heavy
    like a grey cat
        sitting on her chest
            crushing her thin bones

Marta has learnt to gauge by eye
    and not second guess

even when the cat's nails scratch
    at the splinters of sorrow
        its soft pads pushing
            slivers deeper below the breastbone

Marta knows scales cannot measure this
    She has learnt nothing determines how much is enough.

The Marta Poems

What to Do with All That Grief?

Marta saved all her tears
in a little lace-edged handkerchief

night after night she cried
days tiptoed behind lost in the flood

until John said "enough"
and she stopped

folded the handkerchief
into the smallest of squares

a tiny chest full of tears which
she buried in the bottom of one of her drawers.

Resting

somewhere between winter and spring,
lost in a sea of black dresses.

Silk billows like dark waves wrapping
against the lonely house.

A year has passed. A year of mourning and
Marta has run out of black dresses.

She gathers scraps of velvet, cotton, felt, anything
that can be sewn between the feathers she has collected.

Ravens' wings flattened and broad
span across her back, a cloak to wrap her sadness.

Wing tips reaching and meeting
to clasp around shrunken bones,

the slightest hint of blue against pale skin,
veins of a feather piercing her bones.

When this dress wears out, she begins to save everything dark.
Shards of conversation, bitter memories of what was done,

what wasn't, sewn together to make a new dress. To make a dress
that will become her favourite, the one she will wear every day.

Making Plans

The rain has fallen steadily since early morning.
It pools around the terracotta pot left out all winter.
It collects in the ruts where ice has damaged the path.
Marta has waited for this rain,

for this spring, but now April is here,
she is tired from grey pressing on bones
already aching from the long winter
and what death has stolen from her.

Stuck inside she plans the garden,
brambles and thorns left to sprawl wildly,
weave around the small house
like a forest in a long-ago fairytale.

Marta gathers herbs to plant, miracles to cure.
Orders seeds to scatter around the yellow rose bush,
St John's Wort and a fringe of lavender and thyme
to put around the peony stalks that she let flop.

In this year of loss Marta is afraid to leave the house,
afraid of losing her way. She shoves breadcrumbs
into pockets just in case, collects pieces of thread,
saves everything to rescue hope.

Even the blue jays slump as the rain continues
to stream, its weight battering her to exhaustion.
The vines flap madly, shaking water from their thorns
Marta wonders if she pricks her finger
could she sleep through it all?

In the Arboretum

among the flowering bushes, the magnolia
and the tree at the top of the hill that will

bulge with pears, Marta chooses a touchstone.
It is beyond the tree with roots shaped like elephant feet,

past the weeping willow, the one with
thick braided fingers that scoops mouthfuls

from the nearby pond, it is down from, and
just to the left of, a row of majestic burr oaks.

She takes all afternoon to choose, hugs tree
after tree makes sure their bark grazes the insides

of her curved arms, makes sure the scratches
run deep leaving a thin scarlet line on white.

When it feels just right she ties a thin piece of string
to the end of the branch so she will never forget.

Resolutions

6 am and Marta sits at the breakfast table
fingers carefully stepping over crumbs

dishes washed and stacked; laundry folded neatly
floors already mopped, though no one is expected

visitors do not come to this house, and nothing
is as still as this morning, the first of the year

Marta sits alone building crumbs
John has said no there will be

                        no more children

in this empty swell of quiet
Marta sculpts crumbs into the scarred wood

By 10, a little girl moulded
from the bread smiles at her

                        small heart beating.

Sewing Again

It is all she can do
all she knows.
She does not enjoy it
but she is good
and people come
to the small house
with minor alterations.

She stitches hems
replaces buttons
fixes zippers
sews together
pieces for others.

It is mostly immigrants
who seek her service
bringing broken pieces
for Marta to mend.

The Lightness of a Grackle

leaves no print pattering
along the tarp that covers

the broken step where John slipped
rain puddle blue gathers in a pool

where a grackle walks on water
the stress of the bird less

than the footprints of her ghost-child
fifty years and the child still glides

through the house, entering
uninvited into dreams and rooms

as Marta wearies through days
minutes crawling behind her

like ribbons on a bonnet quivering
while Irena's footprints press

her ten perfect little toes squeezing
Marta's heart cupping the strings

so gentle they close
and Marta can't let go.

John Fades Away

lying in the hospital
with Marta by his side
broken hip unable to mend
infection swelling through
the lower half of his body.

Hyacinths in a pot, a gift
from neighbours,
drench the room with
heady scent that creeps
along Marta's chest
waking the same scratching
from her years in England.

The weight bewildering
she can't possibly stay.
Marta touches John's hand
the lightness of goodbye
follows as she leaves.

In the waiting room she
pulls a brown leather diary
from her handbag and
with small, precise writing
makes her first entry
in over fifty years.

All the Small Arguments

Marta kept all the small arguments.

She kept them pressed between books
She kept them folded between fresh-laundered sheets
She kept them planted along the side of the stone pathway
She kept them stacked beside cups and saucers
She kept them buried in her handbag
She kept them crushed and scattered with the bird seed
She kept them floating in a water glass beside the bed
She kept them mixed with potash and eggshells
      to sprinkle around the roses
She kept them souring beneath her tongue
She kept them fermenting in jars of preserves
She kept them crushed to her chest.

She kept them all giving them no more notice
than she would the graze of a moth's wing
catching the light

until John died and then
Marta saw what they really were
so she gathered them up
into a tidy package and put them in
the bottom of a small brown leather satchel
that had one broken clasp.

There in the darkness
moths turned to bats
a thousand beating wings
spreading a black velvet cloak
smothering any love she may have had left.

The Marta Poems

The Quiet Years

In these quiet years
Marta sits alone, left
to stitch the pieces
of cloth that she has

collected and saved.
On her bed she spreads
each one. First a small
square from childhood,

the fragment from
her Sunday dress
which when held
against her cheek

still has the slight
whiff of smoke.
She drags the brown
leather satchel from

under the bed and
between its rigid
divides fishes a
frayed lace ribbon,

no longer than
her pinky-finger.
It is the last of the
edging she had once

used to make delicate
handkerchiefs for sale.
Close to the bottom
fingers catch a red patch

of cloth embroidered
with threads of gold
the sharp flecks
tangled around a

scrap of grey linen
still scented by
the deep richness
of sweet cinnamon.

Pressed against
the aged leather
and gummed to
its humid sides

is a tiny piece
of summer dress.
Blue cornflowers
dots in a white sky,

a little girl's petti-
coat, faded perhaps
but flowers still
fresh, never worn.

Marta litters the bed
with the squares,
the lace, the Sunday
best and then between

she weaves ribbons
of black, ripped from
the dress she wore
when Irena was buried.

She makes a pattern
fashions a bedspread
edges the material
with shreds of paper,

secrets from her diary
written years before,
a perfect fringe for the
cover she has waited all

these years to make.
She takes two white
sheets, puts one over,
one under, and wraps

the quilt accordion-
style, lays it in a
cardboard box and
buries it under the bed.

On Sleeping

Marta doesn't sleep well these days
except in the afternoon when the quiet
yellow sun cradles her into a dream
where she sees a man in a long black overcoat.
She fancies the man is a peddler
with a top hat and a beard, wiry as wool
his eyes round as marbles gleaming
eager to sell to a lonely, motherless widow.

In the heart of the quiet sun, sleep keeps Marta soft
and she sees a cart, an old-fashioned wagon laden
with bottles of potions and pills, lace from a bodice,
a comb and the glint of a mirror
wrapped in the dizzy-sweet-scent of apples
blushing rosy-red, cider-tart, bursting crisp and ripe.

Marta wants one. She wants a bite, a bite for her child,
a magic bite to stir the girl who held her breath until
the man in the white overcoat said she was dead.

In the arms of the yellow sun,
Marta reaches for the juiciest apple
the fairest of them all
doesn't realize she's confused and has it all backwards
but once again it's too late and the sun lets go,
dips tangerine behind the houses.
Marta stirs and it's all gone.

No peddler with potions
no magic, no fairy-tale,
no girl-child
just a breath of overripe apples
poisoning the dark.

The Marta Poems

The Marta Poems

Now

The Marta Poems

After Life

The rain hasn't stopped since the night before
and now the cardboard boxes rest,

swollen and blistered,
their innards stuck together.

These coffins I had always wanted to glimpse, gape open,
guzzling the October rain, soaking into every pore.

I want to cry. There it lies - her life.
She's been buried for over two years,

the house now sold, everything outside
and strewn for all to see.

I don't suppose anyone cared about the weather
or what was in those boxes reeking of age and sickness,

her smell, her room, the cloy of it sewn into
airmail envelopes with exotic stamps,

ink running like streaked mascara
down the face of reams of writing.

So much of life lying dead in a piled heap
waiting for the garbage collector.

The Marta Poems

Peeking from the wreckage was their wedding photograph.
The only photograph I'd seen while she was alive.

I took it and wondered what else was still there trying to live.
I couldn't help myself, kept going back, creeping in the dark

pulling the bones of her life from the curb and carrying them
to my basement hoping in time I could add meat and flesh,

breathe life into the whispers of yellowed paper
splayed on my desk till the space was covered.

Envelopes overlapping, one over the other,
envelope on envelope, fanned like wings,

a thousand drowned moths sopping wet and tissue-thin
aching to survive.

Acknowledgements

I would like to thank the following journals and anthologies where a number of these poems first appeared: *The Antigonish Review, Arc Magazine, After the Book Store Closes for the Night,* an anthology published by *Bondi Studios, Inwords Refug(e)e Special Anthology, League of Canadian Poets, Heartwood Anthology, Greens Magazine, ottawater* and *Room Magazine.*

Thank you, also, to several selection and contest committees. A suite, from an earlier version of the manuscript was shortlisted for the *Exile's* 2016 *Gwendolyn MacEwen Award,* a section of different poems was a finalist for the 2016 *Tree Chapbook Contest* and several of the poems were chosen by *The Sawdust Reading Series Poem-Off Competition.*

My thanks to The Ontario Arts Council for grants that gave financial assistance while writing parts of this book. With gratitude, thank you to *Arc Magazine, Guernica Press, Palimpsest Press* and *The New Quarterly,* for seeing the potential and supporting the manuscript through the OAC Recommender Grant Program.

A bouquet of thanks to my fellow poets from both The Other Tongues Poetry group and the dear Ruby Tuesdays Writers Group. With your expertise, passion, support and suggestions you have helped more than words can say.

Gratitude to Candice James, publisher and editor, who believed in the manuscript from the beginning and took that belief and transformed it into a book. Thank you, thank you, thank you.

I offer my heartfelt thanks to Rhonda Douglas, great mentor and friend, who read the manuscript in all its drafts and helped shape Marta's journey into a story. Without your ongoing support and advice, *Marta's bones may still be lying in cardboard boxes.* Thank you.

And it is with all my love that I thank my family, Anthony and our daughters Jasmine, Hayley, Abigayle and Tiah and my incredible group of friends. I dedicate this book to you, for all the years that you have cared and supported enough to listen every time I asked, "how does this sound?"

The Marta Poems

Notes

The Marta Poems were borne out of an unlikely friendship between Marta and the Poet, that sprung into hours of storytelling and the sharing of tales. Though Marta was the muse, the inspiration behind the journey with its highlights and shadows, many of the poems have been fictionalized and written as a way to give a universal voice for those who shared Marta's path.

Marieta Brzeski's beautifully written memoir, *Roots and Up Rooting*, lent inspiration and help in authenticating some of Marta's oral histories. It helped shape a timeline and accurate framework and offered reassurance that the journey of a displaced people was widespread, common and mostly ignored. Thank you for adding your voice.

Online sources that bring historical weight to this work of fiction include *"The General Langfitt Story, Chapter 3 – Exile in the USSR", "Evacuation of Polish Civilians from the USSR in World War II", "World War Two, The Deportation of Polish Refugees to Abercorn Camp"* and a Wikipedia Page about Crossing the Caspian Sea.

Afternoon Portrait, page 48, takes its title and form from the William Carlos Williams poem of the same name.

Lover, Beloved, page 53, takes its italicized lines from *"The Perfect Poem"*, written by Heather McHugh

www.ingramcontent.com/pod-product-compliance
Lightning Source LLC
Chambersburg PA
CBHW070931080526
44589CB00013B/1471